Countries of the World

Guatemala

by Michael Dahl

Content Consultant:
Maria Landis
Embassy of Guatemala

Bridgestone Books

an imprint of Capstone Press

Bridgestone Books are published by Capstone Press
818 North Willow Street, Mankato, Minnesota 56001
http://www.capstone-press.com

Library of Congress Cataloging-in-Publication Data
Dahl, Michael S.
    Guatemala/by Michael Dahl.
    p. cm.--(Countries of the world)
    Includes bibliographical references and index.
    Summary: Discusses the history, landscape, people, animals, food, sports, and culture
of the country of Guatemala.
    ISBN 1-56065-738-3
    1. Guatemala--Juvenile literature. [1. Guatemala.]
I. Title. II. Series: Countries of the world (Mankato, Minn.)
F1463.2.D34   1998
972.81--dc21

                            97-44465
                              CIP
                              AC

Editorial credits:
Editor, Christy Steele; cover design, Timothy Halldin; interior graphics, James Franklin;
   photo research, Michelle L. Norstad

Photo credits:
Capstone Press, 5 (left)
Maxine Cass, 18
International Stock/Greg Johnston, 6, 12
Byron Jorjorian, 14
Ann Littlejohn, 5 (right), 10
Rob Outlaw, 16, 20
Branson Reynolds, cover, 8

Table of Contents

Name: Republic of Guatemala
Capital: Guatemala City
Population: More than 11 million
Languages: Spanish, Mayan
Religion: Mostly Roman Catholic

Size: 42,042 square miles
  (109,309 square kilometers)
Guatemala is about the size of the U.S. state of Ohio.
Crops: Coffee, sugar, bananas, corn

Maps

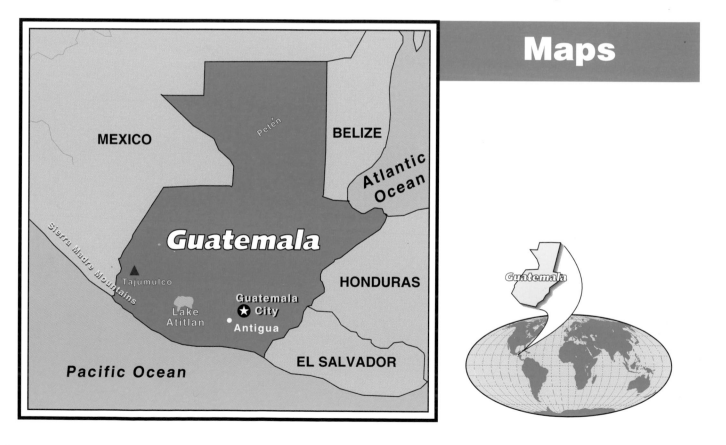

4

Flag

Guatemala's flag has a light blue stripe on each of its ends. There is a white stripe in its middle. A drawing appears on the white stripe. It shows a red and green quetzal (ket-SAHL). The quetzal is Guatemala's national bird. Next to the quetzal is a paper. The paper says Liberty, 15 September 1821. That was when Guatemala became an independent country. Before that, it belonged to Spain.

Currency

The unit of currency in Guatemala is the quetzal. It is named after Guatemala's national bird.

About six quetzals equal one U.S. dollar.

The Land of Guatemala

Guatemala is the third largest country in Central America. It is south of Mexico. Guatemala's borders touch the Pacific and Atlantic Oceans.

Mountains cover three-fourths of Guatemala. The Sierra Madre is one of its major mountain ranges. Guatemala also has highlands and lowlands. Rain forests and huge farms called fincas (FEENK-ahs) cover the lowlands.

Guatemala has 34 volcanoes. A volcano is a mountain with a hole in its middle. Sometimes volcanoes erupt. At these times, lava flows out of the volcanoes. Lava is hot, melted rock. Tajumulco (Tah-hoo-MUL-koh) is one of Guatemala's volcanoes. It is also the highest mountain in Central America.

Guatemala's warm weather keeps flowers and trees growing all year. Guatemalans call their country the land where it is always spring.

Guatemala has 34 volcanoes.

7

Guatemalan People

Mayan Indians were the first people to live in Guatemala. Long ago, Mayan people built stone cities and temples. Today, the remains of these cities and temples still stand. Many people come to Guatemala to see these remains.

Mayan people make up 53 percent of Guatemala's population. There are 23 Mayan Indian groups. Most Mayan families live in small villages and farms. Others live in large cities.

In the 1500s, Spanish explorers came to Guatemala from Spain. They fought the Mayan people and took over Guatemala. Some Spaniards married Mayan Indians and raised families. Ladinos (lah-DEE-nohs) are relatives of these people. They are both Spanish and Mayan. Ladinos live mainly in cities.

People from the Caribbean Islands also moved to Guatemala. Black Caribs are people who came from the Caribbean Islands.

Mayan people make up 53 percent of the population.

Going to School

About 75 percent of Guatemalan children go to school. Children attend school from age seven through 14.

Primary-school students learn reading, Spanish, math, and science. In city schools, children also learn to speak French and English.

Rural schools stay open from January to October. Rural means away from large cities and towns. The school day lasts only four hours. Village children go home after school and help with chores. City schools have seven-hour school days.

Many Guatemalan teenagers leave high school to work. Some teenagers attend secondary school. Students can choose to learn job skills at secondary school.

Some students continue their education in college. College is a school people go to after high school.

About 75 percent of Guatemalan children go to school.

Guatemalan Food

Maize and beans are the main foods of Guatemalan people. Maize is a kind of corn.

People crush maize into powder. They mix the powder with water to make tortillas. A tortilla is a flat bread made out of corn. People fill tortillas with fried beans or meat. Guatemalan people may eat tortillas several times a day.

Enchiladas are tortillas filled with meat, cheese, and spicy sauce. Enchiladas are popular among Black Carib families.

People in cities buy their food at grocery stores. People in rural areas buy their food at outdoor markets. They can buy tacos, cashew nuts, bananas, and corn fritters. A fritter is a small cake.

The zapote (zuh-POH-tay) is a favorite Guatemalan fruit. It grows on the chicle (CHIK-lay) tree. People make chewing gum with sap from the chicle tree.

People in rural areas buy their food at outdoor markets.

Animals in Guatemala

Many kinds of animals live in Guatemala's jungles. A jungle is land covered with trees, vines, and bushes. Spider monkeys climb on tree branches. Yellow jaguars hunt on the ground.

Colorful birds also live in the jungles. The quetzal is a favorite kind of bird. The quetzal has bright green and scarlet feathers. Gold feathers crown its head. The quetzal's tail can grow more than three feet (90 centimeters) long. Some postage stamps from Guatemala have pictures of quetzals on them.

Scarlet macaws and toucans also live in Guatemala. Macaws are long-tailed parrots. Toucans are birds with long, curved beaks. Their beaks are as long as their bodies.

Manatees swim along Guatemala's eastern coast. Manatees look like overgrown seals. Sometimes people call them sea cows.

Scarlet macaws live in Guatemala.

Homes and Clothing

Many people in Guatemala dress like people from North America. They live in houses that are similar to North American houses. But Mayan people have kept their own way of life.

Mayan women and girls wear colorful, loose blouses called huipils (WEE-pils). They also wear long, striped skirts called cortes (KORE-tayss). Many Mayan women tie sashes around their waists. Sashes are long strips of cloth. Both men and women wear head coverings called tzutes (ZOO-tayss).

At home, Mayan women weave cloth. Weave means to pass threads over and under each other. The women cover the cloth with colorful patterns and decorations. The decorations tell stories about their families or villages.

At home, Mayan women weave cloth.

Sports and Outdoors

Soccer is the most popular sport in Guatemala. Both boys and girls practice soccer at school. Children also play basketball and baseball.

Guatemalan people enjoy riding bikes and horses. They often take part in horse and bike races. Successful bike racers are famous in Guatemala. They visit major cities and towns.

Guatemalans and visitors enjoy climbing the mountains. People ride boats down rivers. Lake Atitlan (ah-TEET-lahn) is a popular lake. Many people travel there for swimming and boating.

Petén is in northern Guatemala. It is a large area covered with jungles. The jungles hide the remains of many Mayan buildings. Petén is also full of caves. Some people visit the Mayan ruins. Others explore the caves.

Some people visit the Mayan ruins.

Holidays

Every year, Guatemalans enjoy a holiday called Carnival. Children make cascarones (cah-skah-ROH-nees). Cascarones are painted eggs filled with confetti. Confetti is small pieces of colored paper. Children crack the eggs over people's heads at Carnival parties.

Holy Week is the most important holiday in Guatemala. People celebrate Holy Week between Palm Sunday and Easter Sunday. Schools close and adults stop working. In the city of Antigua (an-TEE-gwah), people march in religious parades. Colorful pictures cover the streets. People make the pictures out of colored sawdust and flower petals.

Musicians play marimba (mah-RIM-bah) music on special days. A marimba is a musical instrument. It looks like a large, wooden xylophone. Marimbas are so large that several people can play one together.

People make pictures on the street for Holy Week.

Hands On: Make a Cascarone

Children in Guatemala make cascarones for Carnival. You can make a cascarone, too.

What You Need

A hollow, plastic egg   Scissors
Sheets of colored paper   Glue
Ribbon or lace   Glitter

What You Do

1. Cut some of the colored paper into little pieces. Ask an adult to help you. This will be your confetti. Put the confetti inside the egg.
2. Decide how you want to decorate your egg. Glue glitter, ribbon, and lace to your egg. Cut shapes from the remaining colored paper and glue them on the egg.
3. Let the glue dry.

You now have a cascarone. You can sprinkle confetti on people you know. Guatemalans call their confetti pica pica (PEE-kah PEE-kah). This means itch itch in English. They call it this because the confetti itches.

Learn to Speak Spanish

boy	niño	(NEEN-yoh)
food	comida	(koh-MEE-dah)
girl	niña	(NEEN-yah)
good bye	adios	(ah-dee-OHS)
good morning	buenos dias	(bway-nohs DEE-ahs)
hello	hola	(OH-lah)
house	casa	(KAH-sah)
thank you	gracias	(GRAH-see-ahs)

Words to Know

confetti (kuhn-FET-ee)—small pieces of colored paper

jungle (JUHNG-guhl)—land covered with trees, vines, and bushes

marimba (mah-RIM-bah)—a large wooden instrument

tortilla (tor-TEE-yah)—a flat bread made out of corn

volcano (vol-KAY-noh)—a mountain with a hole in its middle

quetzal (ket-SAHL)—a red and green bird that is the national bird of Guatemala

Read More

Brill Targ, Marlene and Richard Targ. *Guatemala*. Enchantment of the World. Minneapolis: Children's Press, 1993.

Malone, Michael. *A Guatemalan Family*. Minneapolis: Lerner Publications, 1996.

Useful Addresses and Internet Sites

Embassy of Guatemala
2220 R Street NW
Washington, DC 20008

Guatemala Unlimited
P.O. Box 786
Berkeley, CA 94701

Guatemala Connection
http://www.guateconnect.com/
Guatemala Web Pages
http://mars.cropsoil.uga.edu/trop-ag/guatem.htm

Index